An Intelligent Mind is a Criminal Mind

A short book
By

DR SANJEEV DAVEY

i

This book conceptualized on Intelligence role in a criminality ; can help both students at undergraduate as well as Post graduate levels in Forensic Science, Psychology, Criminology as well psychiatry field, to understand some of bewildering aspects of crime and intelligence association. The readers will get thought provoking researchable areas in this field after reading this book.

ISBN-13: 978-1515088684

ISBN-10: 1515088685

DEDICATION

This book on " **An intelligent mind is a criminal mind** " is dedicated to my late **mother- Asha Davey**, whose hard work I cannot forget in my life along with my constant supporter my **father- Shri Venayack Ram Davey**, whose efforts I cannot forget in my life; without their presence and motivation this book, would not have emerged.

But I am really extremely thankful to my **Wife: DR. Anuradha Davey** who has given a real direction in my life and my 3 children and my **In-laws** efforts for giving me a time to write this book.

Lastly I finally thank **god** for inspiring me to write this book.

CONTENTS

ACKKNOWLEDGMENTS

Author Dr. Sanjeev Davey is very thankful to all the Institutions and his teachers, for their valuable teaching, quite right from the time he joined MBS, MD in CHA as well as during his tenure as Asstt. Prof in Medical colleges of India, because of which this book was possible.

1ST CHAPTER

INTELLIGENCE-CRIME -SCENARIO

INTELLIGENCE -has been defined in many ways such as it is the one's capacity for logic, abstract-thought, understanding, self-awareness, communication, learning, emotional-knowledge, memory, planning, creativity and problem solving as per Wikipedia dictionary[2015]. [1] The term **crime** denotes any unlawful activity done, which punishable by a state.

Intelligence is seen at the highest level in humans, although it is also observed in animals, plants & in machines e.g. artificial intelligence is shown by software's. [1] Infact intelligence is something, which makes people to understand, comprehend analyze and act according to given situations. Intelligence is just like a balance, where its waxing and waning on higher or lower level is both troublesome. The psychometric approach in intelligence is the most researched and by far the most widely used in practical settings.[1]

In the current era of Materialistic world with budding Polished crime, intelligence seems to be playing a dominant role. As more Intellectuals, Businessman , Politicians & Beaurocrats are getting involved in heronious crimes all across the Let us see how intelligence is associating with crime across the world, nowadays.

3

2ᴺᴰ CHAPTER

RELATIONSHIP OF INTELLIGENCE & CRIME

Intelligence and crime are often associated with each other. The relationship between intelligence and crime is complex. This remains a less understood area among normal people vs criminals. [2] It has been found that persons with low average functioning in cognitive impairments are often found within the prisons.[3]

But this may not be always true, as nowadays more intelligent people are also indulging in crimes as evinced by newspaper and TV reports. The reason which might be responsible may be impatience percolating in genes from generations to generations apart from lust to lead to a more luxurious life. Therefore people want to follow an easy path for there life, hence they are more resorting to crimes, even despite having good intelligence.

It has been further seen that the association between intelligence and delinquency have substantial residual confounding. Studies also suggest that there is an association between general cognitive ability and violent criminality.[4] Further the association between psychosis and criminality is indirect one and it is mediated through an illness-related increased vulnerability for general criminogenic factors as poverty, social deprivation and substance abuse, which gets intensified by deficits of modern mental health care. [5]

3RD CHAPTER

PSYCHIATRIC MORBIDITIES ROLE IN INTELLIGENCE & CRIME

It has also been seen from a study in Switzerland that substance abuse was found in 50% of all men in both groups of major mental disorders, and substance abusers had twice as high a probability of having a criminal record. The violent criminality has also been found in schizophrenic patients without comorbid substance abuse, and patients with affective disorders without substance abuse had a higher probability of committing crimes against property. Men with major mental disorder also have an increased probability of becoming criminal even when there is no comorbid substance abuse. [6]

It has also been seen that the 1% of the population are accountable for more than 60% of all violent crime convictions .It has also been seen further that -the majority of violent crimes are perpetrated by a small number of persistent violent offenders, typically males, characterized by early onset of violent criminality, substance abuse, personality disorders, and nonviolent criminality. [7]

4TH CHAPTER

The Correlation Between IQ & Crime

Many facets of a criminal lifestyle can impair cognitive abilities, including physical injuries, especially head traumas, drug use, and withdrawing from school. It is also possible that low IQ may be increasing criminal behavior, criminal behavior might be decreasing IQ, so they are correlated.[8]

The most widely accepted explanation of the IQ-crime correlation is that of *school-performance hypothesis* which states that Less intelligent students do less well in school, which results in academic frustration. This frustration, in turn, weakens their attachment and commitment to schooling, and a weakened bond to school, as per social control theory, allows for more criminal behavior. [8]

A more recent, and more compelling, causal explanation emphasizes the importance of intelligence—especially verbal intelligence—during childhood socialization. The socialization of children involves constant verbal communication and comprehension of abstract symbols; therefore, children with poor verbal and cognitive skills have greater difficulty completing the socialization process, which puts them at risk of under-controlled, antisocial behavior. Empirical studies overall have supported this developmental hypothesis, and it fits with the especially strong correlation between verbal IQ and crime.[8]

In between the two extremes, more sensible interpretation of the IQ-crime correlation appears moderately strong.[9] In 1994, Herrnstein and Murray had published their highly controversial book *The Bell Curve* in which they argued, that racial differences in crime rates resulted from racial differences in intelligence.[9] Literatures also suggest that Delinquents and criminals average IQ scores 8 to 10 points lower than noncriminals, which is about one-half a standard deviation. IQ and criminal behavior are negatively correlated at about r = -.20. [9]

There are two different types of IQ measures: performance IQ (PIQ) versus verbal IQ (VIQ). Performance IQ is measured with nonverbal tests of attention to detail, manual design construction, and visual puzzle solving. Verbal IQ is measured with tests of general factual knowledge, abstract reasoning, mental arithmetic, and vocabulary. [9]

Studies have consistently found that criminals have PIQ scores close to the general population but VIQ scores substantially lower. This PIQ > VIQ finding holds even when controlling for race, class, and reading ability (Moffitt), suggesting that verbal intelligence is a more important correlate of criminal behavior than other types of intelligence. [9]

Other explanation given by few critics are also that, the poor commit more crime because they choose to. The lack of moral teaching, breakdown of family structure and cyclical use of social benefits as opposed to a strong work ethic lead to lower IQ and crime.

5ᵗʰ CHAPTER

1. Terrie Moffitt and colleagues studied 4,552 Danish men born at the end of World War II and found that the men who committed two or more criminal offenses by 20 years had IQ scores on average a full standard deviation below nonoffenders, and IQ and criminal offenses were significantly and negatively correlated at $r = -.19$. [9]

2. Donald Lynam and colleagues studied 430 seventh-grade boys in Pittsburgh, Pennsylvania. They measured both IQ and self-reported participation in delinquent acts and they found that those boys who committed serious delinquent acts, such as stealing cars, breaking and entering, or selling drugs, scored 8–10 IQ points lower than boys who had not. [9]

3. Hakan Stattin and Ingrid Klackenberg-Larsson followed 122 Swedish males from ages three though thirty and found that IQ at age three significantly correlated with registered crime at (Spearman's) rho = $-.25$. IQ at the later ages also correlated with crime at around rho = $-.20$. [9]

4. Scott Menard and Barbara Morse studied 257 high school students in San Diego, California, measuring both IQ and self-reported delinquency and found that IQ was correlated with serious crime—such as gang fights, auto theft, grand

theft, and robbery—at r = -.16. [9]

5. Deborah Denno analyzed data from 987 African American school children in Philadelphia and they found that female chronic offenders were almost four times less likely to be in the top third of verbal-IQ test scores than female non offenders. However male violent offenders scored 10 to 17 percentile points lower on measures of vocabulary, reading, and language than non offenders. [9]

6. Menard and Morse hypothesized also that school teachers and administrators negatively label low-IQ students thus increasing their risk of criminal behavior. In addition to testing this hypothesis, studies should examine other societal reactions to IQ as well. Stories abound of classmates stigmatizing bright students as "brains" and "geeks," especially in schools with overall low scholastic achievement. Bright students might avoid these negative labels by cutting back on schoolwork and acting out antisocially. Indeed, peers' labels of high-IQ students may cause more harm than officials' labels of low-IQ students. [9]

6TH CHAPTER

Role of Intelligence Level in Criminal Behaviour

Criminal behavior is said to occur if it is engaged in by humans, like murder, rape, assault, and theft, are quite common among other species and men with lower intelligence are less likely truly to comprehend evolutionarily novel entities.[10]

Criminologists often feel that criminals on average have lower intelligence than the general population, but they do not know why. Now less intelligent men commit fewer crimes if the police disappear, although more intelligent men may commit more crimes .[10]

The relationship between criminality and intelligence may be considered indirect since criminal tendencies are manifested to a similar degree and with a similar frequency by offenders regardless of intellectual endowment.[11]

Recidivism appears unrelated to the intellectual endowment since it occurs with essentially the same frequency among the mentally deficient offenders as among those of better intellectual capacities.[11]

There appears to be none or slight relationship between the gravity of the offense committed and the degree of intelligence possessed since both high and low grade feebleminded commit crimes as serious as those of their more intellectually gifted fellows.[11]

7TH CHAPTER

Intelligence Shift Across the GLOBE

The developing world is like a different kettle of fish. They're taking off in the way. In America and Britain in 1900, the mean IQ was 70 and then they introduced a bit of formal education, and our IQ went up, and that IQ advance meant that people pursue more formal education. [12]

From the data for about 30 countries, and it falls into the pattern that the gains are greatest — perhaps something like six points a decade — on the culturally reduced tests like Raven's. Next in line are usually the Wechsler performance tests — they go up at about four points a decade — and then finally the verbal tests rise at about two or three points a decade. [12]

Over the past century, the average IQ in industrialized countries has risen to keep pace with the complexity of modern life. [12]

8TH CHAPTER

Why Intelligent People –Committing Crimes: Examples of Polished & White Collar Crimes

The question of what motivates smart and talented people to commit fraud is really very fascinating. Let us see how this is happening in developing countries such as India:

Emerging Era of Polished Crimes:-

The recent newspaper Indian Express(2015,July 13) also shows that the changing face of polished crimes are now in the form of Crisp dressing, a sophisticated air, polite language, smooth talk and a searching eye. [13]

The people with polished crime operate in a manner to seduce you into parting your wealth after gaining your trust, or intimidating with you the swagger and jargon that could put a seasoned bureaucrat to shame. [13] The Polished crime people also pretend as police officers, CBI officers, vigilance and anti-corruption officers, human resources officials - and even as journalists and soothsayers and the so called 'tax officials'. [13]

These days teachers, researchers, Government office bearers, all are moving towards easy money, not doing work of people and fulfilling luxury in their life by doing polished crimes. The changing face of prostitution from brothel houses to a alone house for sex with female are also one form of polished crime.

Rise of White-collar crimes(WCS):-

WCS is the financially motivated nonviolent crime now committed by many business and government Officials & talented professionals such as Doctors, Engineers, Politicians etc.[1] This was first defined by sociologist Edwin Sutherland in 1939 as "a crime committed by a person of respectability and high social status in the course of his occupation". [13]

Typical white-collar crimes include: [13]

1. **Fraud,**

2. **Bribery,**

3. **Ponzi schemes,**

4. **Insider trading,**

5. **Embezzlement,**

6. **Cybercrime,**

7. **Copyright infringement,**

8. **Money laundering,**

9. **Identity theft, and**

10. **Forgery.**

9TH CHAPTER

FEW EXAMPLES OF MOST INTELLIGENT CRIMES

Lets see Most Intelligent crimes committed in Indian context:[14,15]

Indias Securities scam : Harshad Mehta case:

He was an Indian stockbroker who did the notorious BSE security scam of 1991. IT department has itself admitted that they are still unaware of how much money Harshad Mehta engulfed during this scam .

Mithilesh Kumar Srivastava [Natwarlal (1912-2009)]:

An Indian Con Man known for having repeatedly "sold" the Taj Mahal, the Red Fort, and the Rashtrapati Bhavan and also the Parliament House of India along with its 545 sitting members.

Devinder singh aka bunty aka superchor

A compulsive thief, Devinder Singh aka Bunty's was a class nine dropout and he began his life of notoriety in 1993 when he was arrested in New Delhi but gave police the slip.

Dawood Ibraham,

The real Don, is infact a true genius has many such tactics up his   sleeves.

Stamp Paper Scam : Abdul Karim Telgi

Abdul Karim Telgi is a convicted Indian counterfeiter. He earned money by printing counterfeit stamp paper in India.

Opera House Burglary (The Special 26) -- Mohan singh

The Bollywood movie Special 26 was inspired by a real life crime, but the plot of the movie was a little different from the original crime. The main difference is that the robbery was not committed by a gang of 4-people, but just a single man.

Ketan Parekh single-handedly run the bull on the share market

Ketan Parekh was a chartered accountant by profession and used to manage a family business, NH Securities started by his father. Known for maintaining a low profile, Ketan Parekh's only dubious claim to fame was in 1992, when he was accused in the stock exchange scam. He was known as the 'Bombay Bull'.

Examples of Current Polished Crimes Across the world

Institutions getting approvals from regulatory authorities such as TRAI by Mobile Phone companies, MCI by Private Medical colleges, Shopkeepers bribing food inspectors, after offering bribe to them.

Emerging face of Crime

The most popular view is now that crime is a category created by law; in other words, something is a crime if declared as such by the relevant and applicable law, if you are caught.

10TH CHAPTER

CONCLUSION

Intelligence refers to intellectual functioning. intelligence quotients, or IQ tests, compare your performance with other people your age who take the same test. But social intelligence is different, the expertise people bring to their interactions with others. there are also generational differences in the population as a whole. better nutrition, more education and other factors have resulted in IQ improvements for each generation.

But improvement in IQ have also lead to people adopting polished crime from top levels to the bottom level. Now it is clearly emerging that even more intelligent people are committing crimes in a modern and highly sophisticated way- so that they do not get caught. Intelligent crimes often go unnoticed/un cracked, as these are done by so called people with good name, fame and money.

What can be concluded is three is boom in white-collar and polished crimes in different shapes and forms, with societies shifting towards hidden crimes by the so called famous people. This has a great implication of destroying morality and propagating the crimes across the world. Therefore so called modern society is turning criminal.

So more Intelligent people are committing crimes as opposed to old view that only persons with low intelligence commit crimes. This area needs further better understanding by researchers working in this area.

References:

1. Neisser, U.; Boodoo, G.; Bouchard, T. J. , J.; Boykin, A. W.; Brody, N.; Ceci, S. J.; Halpern, D. F.; Loehlin, J. C.; Perloff, R.; Sternberg, R. J.; Urbina, S. "Intelligence: Knowns and unknowns". *American Psychologist* 1996;51 (2): 77.

2. JM Miller - 2013. 21st Century Criminology: A Reference Handbook – Sage. Available from: .www.sagepub.com/schram/study/materials/reference/90851_04.2r.pdf.

3. Freeman James. The relationship between lower intelligence, crime and custodial outcomes: a brief literary review of a vulnerable group. WORKING LIFE STRESS, REHABILITATION COUNSELLING AND INCLUSION. Vol 3 (2012) incl Supplements.

4. Frisell T, Pawitan Y, Långström N.Is the association between general cognitive ability and violent crime caused by family-level confounders? PLoS One. 2012;7(7):e41783. Epub 2012 Jul 24.

5.Schanda H.Investigating the association between psychosis and criminality/violence.[Article in German] Fortschr Neurol Psychiatr. 2006 Feb;74(2):85-100.

6. Modestin J, Wuermle O.Criminality in men with major mental disorder with and without comorbid substance abuse. Psychiatry Clin Neurosci. 2005 Feb;59(1):25-9.

7.Falk O, Wallinius M, Lundström S, Frisell T, Anckarsäter H, Kerekes N.The 1% of the population accountable for 63% of all violent crime convictions. Soc Psychiatry Psychiatr Epidemiol. 2014 Apr;49(4):559-71. Epub 2013 Oct 31.

8. IQ –crime Correlation. Available from: http://law.jrank.org/pages/1365/Intelligence-Crime-Explaining-IQ-crime-correlation.html

9. WRIGHT B. R. E. Intelligence and CrimeEncyclopedia of Crime and Justice | **2002** | WRIGHT. Available from: http://www.encyclopedia.com/doc/1G2-3403000143.html.

10. Satoshi Kanazawa .Why Criminals Are Less Intelligent than Non-Criminals. **Available from: https://www.psychologytoday.com/blog/the-scientific-fundamentalist/201006/why-criminals-are-less-intelligent-non-criminals. Last Updated: Jun 27, 2010.**

11.Milton Hylan Erickson, Study of the Relationship Between Intelligence and Crime, A, 19 Am. Inst. Crim. L. & Criminology 592 (1928-1929).

12.Lea Winerman. Smarter than ever? http://www.apa.org/monitor/2013/03/smarter.aspx.

13. U Tejonmayam .More Brain than Brawn as Crime Gets Polished. Available from: http://www.newindianexpress.com/cities/chennai/More-Brain-than-Brawn-as-Crime-Gets-Polished/2014/04/28/article2193241.ece. - CHENNAI. Published: 28th April 2014 07:17 AM. Last Updated: 28th April 2014 07:17 AM

14. Aquinas, Thomas. (1988). *On Law, Morality and Politics*. 2nd edition. Indianapolis: Hackett Publishing Co. ISBN 0-87220-663-7

15. Attenborough, F. L. (ed. and trans.) (1922). *The Laws of the Earliest English Kings.* Cambridge: Cambridge University Press. Reprint March 2006. The Lawbook Exchange, Ltd. ISBN 1-58477-583-1

ABOUT THE AUTHOR

Dr. Sanjeev Davey is an Assistant Professor in the Department of Community Medicine, Muzaffarnagar Medical College, Muzaffarnagar, Uttar Pradesh (India). Dr Sanjeev Davey is also a Public health expert with more than 10 years field experience. He has strong academic background i.e. MBBS, MD (CHA), UGC NET(CH).

He is also a member of prominent Community Medicine and Public health Associations of India such MIAPSM, MIPHA, MACHHA. He has also held position of Associate editor in journals such as - NJRCM, and he is also a Member Advisory Editorial Board of journals such as - MRC, DJIF, JMSCR. He has also done -Reviewer work for journals such as -JCDR., IJMEDPH, IJCH. He has published 35 publications in Indexed journals of International and National repute.

He has also served International Organizations like WHO as SMO in NPSP Project. He also has a good experience in Handling International Research Projects. He has also carried out many qualitative psychological researches in public health field.

www.ingramcontent.com/pod-product-compliance
Lightning Source LLC
Chambersburg PA
CBHW070457290526
45791CB00005B/2147